Zen Wisdom
for the Anxious

Zen Wisdom
for the Anxious

Simple Advice from
a Zen Buddhist Monk

Shinsuke Hosokawa

Illustrated by
Ayako Taniyama

TUTTLE Publishing

Tokyo | Rutland, Vermont | Singapore

Published by Tuttle Publishing, an imprint of Periplus Editions (HK) Ltd.

www.tuttlepublishing.com

Copyright © 2018 Shinsuke Hosokawa

Original Japanese edition published under the title
MAYOI GA KIERU ZEN NO HITOKOTO by Sunmark Publishing, Inc., Tokyo, Japan in 2018. English translation rights arranged through Japan UNI Agency Inc., Tokyo.

English translation © 2020 Periplus Editions (HK) Ltd. English translation by Makiko Itoh.

LCCN 2020944319

ISBN 978-4-8053-1573-6

Printed in Malaysia

TUTTLE PUBLISHING® is a registered trademark of Tuttle Publishing, a division of Periplus Editions (HK) Ltd.

Distributed by:

North America, Latin America & Europe
Tuttle Publishing
364 Innovation Drive
North Clarendon
VT 05759 9436, USA
Tel: 1(802) 773 8930
Fax: 1(802) 773 6993
info@tuttlepublishing.com
www.tuttlepublishing.com

Asia Pacific
Berkeley Books Pte Ltd
3 Kallang Sector #04-01
Singapore 349278
Tel: (65) 6741-2178
Fax: (65) 6741-2179
inquiries@periplus.com.sg
www.tuttlepublishing.com

Japan
Tuttle Publishing
Yaekari Building, 3rd Floor
5-4-12 Osaki Shinagawa-ku
Tokyo 141 0032 Japan
Tel: 81 (3) 5437 0171
Fax: 81 (3) 5437 0755
sales@tuttle.co.jp
www.tuttle.co.jp

27 26 25 24 23
12 11 10 9 8 7 6
2307TO

Contents

What does it mean to "live"?

When we are tossed around by the demands of everyday life, barraged by information from all sides, our spirits lose the room to breathe. We become dissatisfied with our lives, envious of others. At these times, it's important to stop and take a good look at ourselves. The Zen Buddhist quotes in this book will help erase doubts and anxiety and return serenity to your soul.

Although Zen Buddhism may seem remote or unapproachable, its basic philosophy can be summed up as "the knowledge needed to live life with a positive outlook." There are 52 Zen sayings in this book, corresponding not just to the seasons of the year and of our lives, but, in the world of Buddhism, to the 52 stages that lead to enlightenment.

The spacious design of this book relates to the Japanese concept of *ma*, which means pause, silence and space. Alongside each of the 52 sayings, you'll find a few carefully chosen words of interpretation and an illustration that emphasizes *ma*. This word also means "encounter." I hope that you, the reader, will cherish any encounters your heart may make when you reflect on the Zen sayings in this book.

Zen monks like myself often use the moon as a metaphor for enlightenment. These sayings are like fingers pointing toward that moon. However, the important thing is to focus on your own heart rather than the pointing fingers, and to accept your current state of being, your "you." Once you have completed your journey through these 52 Zen sayings, what kind of moon will be shining in your heart?

This is the start of that journey. Feel the quiet light in your heart as you begin to think more deeply about what it means to "live."

—Shinsuke Hosokawa

Prologue

不立文字
ふりゅうもんじ

教外別伝
きょうげべつでん

Words cannot tell everything,
teaching cannot teach everything.

Some things are only
communicated soul to soul.

Value what is passed from heart to heart.

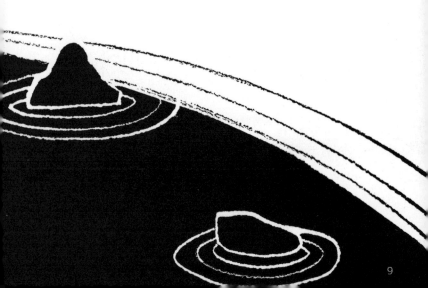

Don't get caught up in words and phrases.

Rise above those words and phrases and
instead, value the things
that you feel in your heart and your soul.

Zengo, the language of Zen Buddhism,
is simply a guide for living.

Truth is to be found in our everyday lives.
It exists in our natural surroundings.

Listen to that voice of truth.

Make small waves in your heart
and be conscious of those waves.

Take time to go exploring
for the truth about life.

Spring

一期一会

いちごいちえ

Treasure every moment,
for it will not come again.

*Your greatest treasures
are right there in front of you.*

Life is a series of encounters.

We encounter people.
We also encounter, books, movies,
physical objects and landscapes.

We are all repeatedly encountering
things that pass before us.

*Encounters happen constantly,
but each occurs only once.*

*It is only when we remember this in our
hearts that we can truly embrace the
connections that encounters make possible.*

Be grateful for each encounter.

*Be thankful when someone or something
reveals itself to us.*

*Treasuring each unique moment gives us
the power to truly live that moment
more meaningfully.*

天上天下唯我独尊

てんじょう てんげ ゆいがどくそん

As the Heavens are above and
the Earth is below,
I was born a human being,
whose existence cannot change.

My life is precious as it is.

All things that exist in this world are precious.

From the Heavens above us to the
deepest parts of this Earth,
all living things are precious.

I am an irreplaceable living being.
And all other living beings are irreplaceable.

Each person is important.
Each thing is important.

Ourselves; our parents; our friends;
dogs and cats; insects and birds;
the pillars that hold up our homes;
the flowers blooming in the flower pots;
the green trees we can see
from our windows.

啐啄同時<ruby>そ<rt></rt></ruby>

そったくどうじ

There is no time like now.

Encounters are never a coincidence.

When an unborn chick pecks at the shell of the egg from the inside at the same time as the mother hen pecks at the egg from the outside, a new life is born.

There are no coincidences in encounters. Encounters are all inevitable.

Thus are our lives renewed.

*Whether we encounter good things
or whether we encounter bad things,
all encounters are inevitable.*

*Good things generously help our
dreams unfold, and bad things
are simply life's small trials.*

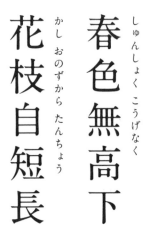

春色無高下　しゅんしょく こうげなく

花枝自短長　かし おのずから たんちょう

The spring sunshine falls
equally on all the flowers,
yet some are taller
than others.

*As long as you have your "self,"
you do not need to concern
yourself with others.*

Spring arrives everywhere, but there
are some cherry blossoms that bloom
early and others that bloom late.

Some cherry blossoms form short
stems, while others form long ones.
Yet what is gained by comparing them?

Early or late blossoms; attractive or
not-so-attractive blossoms;
short or long stems: all are fine.

Even if they differ, cherry blossoms are cherry blossoms. As long as each flower blooms as best as it can, that is fine.

Over your life, you will observe differences between you and others. But what is gained by comparing yourself to them?

Even if there are differences, other people are not you. You are you.

Live your life as best you can, and don't get distracted by trivial things.

白馬入蘆花
はくばろかにいる

A white horse disappears in
a field of white flowers,
but that does not mean it is gone.

*As long as you focus
on what is in front of you,
you will always find your way.*

Even if there is another that is similar to you, you are still unique, an individual.

Keep that thought in your heart and embrace the situation you face. Become the white horse that blends into the field of white flowers.

Instead of always insisting that you are a different color, instead of insisting that your colors are brighter, instead of always asserting yourself, try to not disturb the calm.

Throw your entire self into the field of flowers.

Strive to do what is difficult and disagreeable,
until you and your surroundings blend
into each other without borders.

By doing this, your way will
become clear to you.

When you try as hard as you can,
a path is created.

You will be able to see the way.

冷暖自知
<ruby>冷<rt>れい</rt></ruby><ruby>暖<rt>だん</rt></ruby><ruby>自<rt>じ</rt></ruby><ruby>知<rt>ち</rt></ruby>

Is the water hot or cold?
You can find out for yourself.

Just try it out.

You can find out whether water is cold or warm by touching it yourself.

Don't just wait aimlessly for people to explain things to you. You will end up living inside your head, stalled in one place, letting opportunities slip past.

When you are uncertain, start by trying things out for real, by yourself.

Rather than regretting never having done something, it's better to try it and then regret it.

Even if you regret it later, there is still the "you" that tried, and your "self" will be different compared to before.

It's fine to regret doing something.

It's fine.

掬水月在手
弄花香満衣

みずをきくすれば　つきてにあり
はなをろうすれば　かえにみつ

If you put your hands in water, you
may catch the moon's reflection.

If you play with the flowers you meet
on your path, their fragrance may
perfume your clothes.

Happiness is right there.

When you scoop up water with your hands,
a beautiful moon is reflected in that water,
and when you touch flowers,
your clothing absorbs their fragrance.

Even if you try to look for happiness,
it does not have a shape.
You cannot see it with your eyes.

But once you start to perform an action,
you can feel happiness as something real.

Sometimes, you may sense never-ending life, even in something with a limited lifespan.

Instead of lamenting that you want happiness brought to you, that you want to see happiness, or that you've never seen happiness, try taking the first step toward it of your own volition.

Just take a look around you — the world is overflowing with things that fill your heart with abundance.

Happiness is something you feel.

Happiness is always right there.

鑊湯無冷処
<ruby>鑊<rt>か</rt></ruby><ruby>湯<rt>く</rt></ruby><ruby>無<rt>と</rt></ruby><ruby>冷<rt>う</rt></ruby>

かくとう れいしょなし

There are no cold spots
in boiling water.

If you are living as fully as you can,
you will have no time to be bored.

There is not a single drop of cold
water in a pot of boiling water.

It is said that a famous tea master always
had a pot of water boiling so that he
could receive anyone with the utmost
hospitality no matter when they called.

Pour your whole heart and soul
into every moment.

This is what it means to have a pure heart.

Simply by living our lives, we are inevitably approaching death.

That's why you must immerse your pure heart into every moment.

There is no time to wait until the boiling water has cooled.

There is no time to idle away.

年年歳歳花相似
歳歳年年人不同

ねんねんさいさい はな あいにたり
さいさいねんねん ひと おなじからず

The flowers bloom every year,
but people do not remain
the same from year to year.

Nothing is permanent; that is life.

The cherry blossoms bloomed again this year, as though nothing has changed. I am standing under the blossoming trees the two of us always enjoyed together. But this year I am alone.

Nothing is certain, and nothing is permanent in life. There is nothing that is unchanging and eternal. You cannot stay young forever and life does not last forever.

That is why we must live in the "now."

Even the cherry trees that bloom every year are not exactly the same as they were last year. They have endured the cold of the winter, and been through much to finally bring forth their flowers.

Even if the flowers only open part of the way, do not complain. The blossoms that we take for granted every year continue to flower due to a succession of miracles.

There is no guarantee that the cherry trees that bloomed this year will do so again next year. In the same way, there is no guarantee that the person next to you will still be there next year.

Look up.
Some blossoms are falling.
Some have not yet bloomed.
Some are just starting to peek out.

They are all beautiful.

百花春至為誰開

ひゃっか はるいたって たがためにか ひらく

The hundreds of flowers
in the spring
do not bloom for anyone.
They just bloom.

Let us bloom, just for this life as it is.

For whom do flowers bloom? They don't bloom for anyone. They don't bloom for any reason. Flowers bloom just to live, to bring forth their life force. Flowers simply live, to live their lives to the fullest.

Our human hearts are moved by their beauty, their resilience and their purity.

So . . . For whom do we live? For what reason do we live? Do we live to be thought of as a great person? To be envied? To be the center of attention?

Just like flowers, we humans simply need to live our lives to the fullest — that is enough.

Nothing else is asked of us.

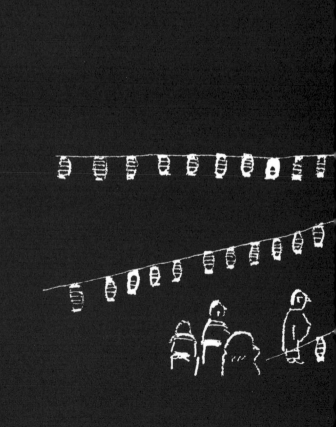

Summer

一日不作 いちにち なさざれば

一日不食 いちにち くらわず

A day without work
is a day without eating.

Eat after your duties have been fulfilled

This famous Japanese saying doesn't mean
"If you don't work you shouldn't eat."
It means if you did not fulfill your duties for
that day, you do not deserve to receive the
nourishment that is provided by another life.

We do not work just to eat.
We work to fulfill our duties.

Every day, we partake of the lives of other
things, in order to continue living ourselves.

We are allowed to live because we each
have our duties to perform in this world.

In order to partake of the lives of other things, we need to consider what we can do to give thanks for those lives.

I am not talking about anything ostentatious, like giving back to society, or being thanked by multitudes. It's about doing what we are doing right now, as best and as wholeheartedly as we can.

That is what is meant by "fulfilling your duties."

Live while fulfilling your duties. We eat every day in order to be able to do this.

Do not just live. Do not just eat.

忘筌 ^{ぼうせん}

Forget about the fishing tackle.
It's the fish that is important.

*Do not confuse the method
with the objective.*

Once you have caught a fish, you can forget about the tool you used to catch it.

Zen meditation and Zen sayings are simply tools for preparing your heart.

The rituals and forms of Zen practice are not important. You don't need to be grateful for them. They are simply tools for achieving enlightenment.

We all quickly forget our beginnings. The sport we took up simply because we enjoyed it.

The hobby we began simply because we found it interesting. We are so easily distracted from those starting points into having the latest sportswear or the best equipment.

Tools are just the means.

*Do not forget the original goal. Don't get
your heart tied up in trivial details.*

*If your heart is getting too tied up,
try throwing away all your tools.*

Return to zero to recover your beginnings.

眼横鼻直

<ruby>眼<rt>がん</rt></ruby> <ruby>横<rt>のう</rt></ruby> <ruby>鼻<rt>び</rt></ruby> <ruby>直<rt>ちょく</rt></ruby>

The nose is in the middle and
the eyes are on either side.

Sometimes we just lose
sight of the truth.

Don't be distracted by the opinions of others, or by your own prejudices.

A person's nose is positioned in the
center of the face. The eyes are on
either side, parallel to each other.

To see obvious facts just for what they are,
and to be able to understand what
is true, takes a long time.

Why is that? It's because people are turned
this way and that by the opinions of others,
or see things through the prism of their own
prejudices, or don't try to see the things in
front of them because they are too busy.

When people do not see what is obviously
true, they do not see the happiness in
front of them, even when it's close.

*A day has a morning, an afternoon
and an evening. A year has a
certain number of seasons.*

*Until we become aware of these obvious
truths and of how blessed we are that these
things exist as they do, we all suffer and
continue to make life difficult for ourselves.*

*It is only once we have made a full
circle and come back to the very place
we started that we become aware of
where happiness is for the first time.*

Happiness is right there.

非風非幡
<ruby>非<rt>ひ</rt></ruby><ruby>風<rt>ふう</rt></ruby><ruby>非<rt>ひ</rt></ruby><ruby>幡<rt>ばん</rt></ruby>

If there is no wind,
the flag does not move.

*The world is not at
fault for bad things.*

A flag is being blown by the
wind and flying in the air.

Is this because the flag is moving?
Or is it because the wind is moving?

No, it's because your heart is moving.

When something happens, we tend to
immediately blame the times we are
living in or the people around us. We
always place responsibility elsewhere
instead of looking inside ourselves.

Don't try to understand this;
just become like the flag.

Do not waver.
Don't be blown about by the wind.
Do not become anxious.
Don't be tossed about by the
people around you.
Look inside yourself, at your own heart.

Truth can always be seen there.

扶過断橋水
伴帰無月村

たすけてはすぐ だんきょうのみず
とものうてはかえる むげつのそん

With support, you can cross
a river with a broken bridge,
and find your way home
on a moonless night.

When you face difficult times,
words of support can help you overcome them.

Life can feel like crossing a river
without a bridge, or like walking in
the darkness on a moonless night.

In difficult times like these, words can
come to your aid. Words can support
you and be your walking cane.

Whenever you feel uncertain and lost,
as long as you have words to support you,
your "unbroken self" can keep going.

Whenever you are in danger of stepping off your path, if there are words that guide you, your "unwavering self" can keep on going.

Keep these words of support close to your heart, and keep pursuing your true self.

What am I?

Keep on asking yourself that question. And then you will be able to move ahead.

珊瑚枕上両行涙
さんごちんじょうりょうぎょうのなみだ

半是思君
なかばはこれきみをおもい

半恨君
なかばはきみをうらむ

As I wait for my lover
on my beautiful bed decorated with coral,
crying into my pillow,
half of me yearns for my love,
half of me curses him.

76

Accept hard words, and use them to feed your heart.

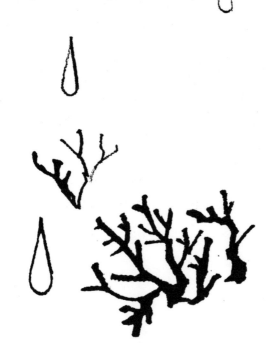

This saying is the lament of a woman waiting for her lover. She cries because she loves him and yet at the same time she hates him.

It is important for people to balance more than one emotion. If you are on the receiving end of criticism, start by accepting it. But instead of being defeated by those harsh words, be grateful toward the other person, and at the same time be angry. Use that anger positively to wake yourself up.

Own those two emotions and take the next step forward.

Don't waste time making excuses.

*Excuses and explanations are
a waste of your heart. There's no
need to harden your own shell.*

Your shell is there for you to break through.

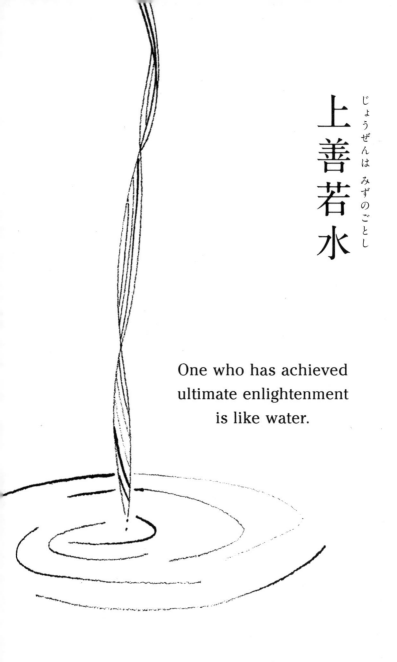

上善は水のごとし

One who has achieved
ultimate enlightenment
is like water.

Life flows like water, endlessly.

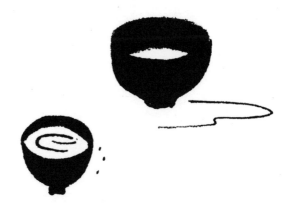

A person who has achieved enlightenment
brings blessings to everything around them,
does not fight with anything, and goes willingly
to places that are shunned by others.

If that enlightened person is put into a
round container they become round,
if put into a square container they become
square. They are able to adapt freely
to each circumstance, like water.

Water flows naturally from a high place
to a low place. That is not because there
is any advantage to it. It's not because
there is some kind of reward for it.

It just flows for its own sake, yet with
enough power to wear away rock.

Flowing water never stops in the same place.
It is perpetually moving, from a
high place to a low place.

People too, should not become fixated
on a particular thing and stop moving.
We should live like flowing water,
without leaving a trace.

If an obstacle presents itself to you,
just divert your flow, and keep going forward.

When you need to, you can gather
enough power within yourself to move
even large obstacles, as you let your
life flow naturally, like water.

This is what it means to live a better life.

与天下人作陰涼

てんかのひとのために　いんりょうとならん

Become a cooling,
shading tree for others.

Making just one other person happy
is in itself happiness.

A large tree spreads its branches and makes shade. As it receives the full, harsh sun of summer, it summons cool breezes and gives respite to those who rest beneath it.

Let us too spread our leaves and create a shade that people can rest under in peace.

Let us too summon a cool breeze that gives others respite.

It's fine to start with small things.
For example, make sure to leave a public
washroom clean after you've used it!

Be someone who makes life a little easier
for someone else, even if you don't know
that person. Be that kind of cooling shade.

You don't have to be that for a multitude;
just be that for one person.

Being of use to someone else
brings joy to your life.

安禅不必須山水
あんぜんはかならずしもさんすいをもちいず

滅却心頭火自涼
しんとうをめっきゃくすれば ひもおのずからすずし

For seated meditation
quiet mountain surroundings
are not necessary.

It is important to overcome
discomfort with your heart.

It's a waste of your spirit to complain about things that you have no control over.

The place where you meditate does not have to be a quiet, pure place. And Zen meditation is not about cooling a burning fire with some kind of supernatural power.

Fire is hot. The ability to accept that heat, and continue living, is the "cool" mentality.

There is no place in this world
that isn't warm or cool.
There is no place that does
not have life and death.

When it's warm, accept the heat,
and when it's cool, accept the chill.

While you are alive, commit to living
and when you die, commit to death.

Don't waste time being pessimistic
and thinking, "I might die."
You are alive right now.

To anticipate and lament hardship that has
yet to happen is a waste of your spirit.

Accept the now as it is, and
concentrate on what is before you,
with a calm body and heart.

There is no need to purposely bring
imagined situations into your life.

香厳撃竹
きょうげんげきちく

The sound of a stone
hitting bamboo
can bring clarity.

Who am I?
Always keep your heart receptive.

Once, long ago, when a Zen monk
called Kyogen was concentrating on
raking the garden, a stone flew and hit
a bamboo trunk, making a sound.
In that instant, it is said that he
realized the answer to who he was.

You cannot know who you are by
listening to the words of others
or from the learning you get from books.
You have to question what is inside your heart.
The answer is inside you.

Keep your heart sharp and alert,
and keep questioning yourself.

What am I living for?
What is the reason for living?
Keep making waves in your heart
as you pursue what is most important.

"Click!"
One day, as a result of some catalyst,
you might just hear that sound inside you.

Fall

廓然無聖
<ruby>廓<rt>かく</rt></ruby><ruby>然<rt>ねん</rt></ruby><ruby>無<rt>む</rt></ruby><ruby>聖<rt>しょう</rt></ruby>

As clear as a cloudless autumn sky.

Do not be bound by anything.

A famous Zen story tells of a warlord during
the Liang Dynasty in China who said to the
great Zen Buddhist monk Daruma,
"I have built many temples until now,
and supported many monks.
Will I obtain much happiness from this?"

The venerable Daruma replied,
"There is no such thing,"

The warlord, dissatisfied with that answer,
asked, "What is the heart of Zen?"

To this the Venerable Daruma
replied, "It's a clear, dry place.
There is no sacred thing there."

The disheartened warlord
asked, "Who are you?"

The Venerable Daruma replied, "I don't know."

*Good deeds are not to be done in
hopes of receiving something in return.*

*Achieving the height of Zen does not mean
that you will go to a sacred place.
All that happens, is that you arrive at
a place where you no longer compare
and contrast things such as sacred
versus profane, or good versus evil.*

"Who am I?"

*We don't know.
The things we don't know,
we keep pursuing.*

That is what it means to live a life.

手放没深泉
てをはなてば　しんせんにぼっす

十方光皓潔
じっぽうひかり　こうけつたり

If I let go I will fall into the water,
and there I will shine
in ten thousand directions.

Do not cling to anything.

A curious monkey was entranced by the moon's reflection in a pool. The monkey held onto a branch with its left hand, and tried to scoop up the moon with its right hand.

If the monkey had let go of the branch to grasp the moon with both hands, it would have fallen into the deep spring for sure. But suddenly the monkey realized that the moon reflected on the surface of the water was a false moon. The real moon was shining brightly in the sky above.

People, too, try to grasp at so many things. Status, fame, reputation, knowledge and experience.

It's impossible to count all the things we hold dear.

Try letting go.

*If you fall into a deep pool, you will flail about.
This time of flailing about is a time of suffering.*

*But from there, when you raise your face from
the water and look up, you can be bathed in
the light of the true moon, not a false one.*

*You can feel the light of the moon that
is known as "true happiness."*

体露金風

<ruby>体<rt>たい</rt></ruby><ruby>露<rt>ろ</rt></ruby><ruby>金<rt>きん</rt></ruby><ruby>風<rt>ぷう</rt></ruby>

Feel the gentle autumn breeze.

Let go of it all.

Under a boundless, cloudless autumn
sky, try feeling a refreshing autumn
breeze with your entire being.

Discard all doubt and worries: the desire to be
promoted, the desire to be famous, the desire
to be praised by others. Throw away all such
greed, and allow your whole being to feel the
refreshing autumn breeze that fills the land.

Look at the golden fields of grain
spread out in front of you.

What is here, now, is just a pure heart that
can see and feel all that is beautiful.

A pure, refreshed heart can
accept what is real.

Discard everything from your life
up until now; the good as well as
the bad. Throw it all away.

When you have done this, enlightenment
will be awakened inside you.

昨夜一声雁
さくやいっせいのかり

清風萬里秋
せいふうばんりのあき

Last night I heard the geese calling.
Fall came before I even noticed.

*At a certain point,
a person realizes the meaning of their life.*

A Buddhist monk in training can achieve enlightenment after a long period of discipline. He is released from his worries at last, and becomes able to feel the cool, pure autumn breeze.

We all worry at one time or another. About work, about our families, about our children, about the future.

But as long as you allow yourself to feel your emotions as you go about your days, sooner or later, you will realize the meaning of your life and your worried heart will be set free.

Then, your heart will become clear and calm.

楓葉経霜紅

ふうようは しもをへて くれないなり

The maple leaves
turn red in the frost.

Life burns brighter in trying times.

The leaves of a maple tree turn a bright, burning red when they are covered by a bone-chilling frost.

Our lives also become richer after experiencing hardship.

If we award ourselves 100 points for fun times in our life, and subtract 100 points for sad times, then our life sum will be zero.

If we award ourselves 100 points for fun times plus 100 points for sad times, then this comes to 200!

After enduring and surviving deep hardship, our lives can reach a period of "bright red leaves."

渓深くして 杓柄長し

<ruby>渓<rt>たに</rt></ruby><ruby>深<rt>ふこ</rt></ruby>うして <ruby>杓<rt>しゃく</rt></ruby><ruby>柄<rt>へい</rt></ruby><ruby>長<rt>ながし</rt></ruby>

To scoop water from far below,
a long handle is needed.

Do not be too obstinate.

Once, a young monk in training asked an elderly monk, "What is the true meaning of Zen?"

The elderly monk replied, "To scoop water from a deep place, a long handle is needed."

If the place is deep and the water is far below, a ladle with a long handle is required to scoop up the water. But if the place is shallow and the water flows close by, a ladle with a short handle is needed.

When you listen to another person, there is no need to deny them, or argue against them. And of course, there is no need to push your "self" on them and be obstinate.

Try dealing with others flexibly, according to their strengths and circumstances.

Try living by adapting yourself to others. Think of what is best for that person.

Try reaching out your hand to others instead of pushing them away.

This is the role of someone who has reached the autumn of their life.

雲無心以出岫
鳥倦飛而知還

くもむしんにしてもって しゅうをいで
とりとぶにうんで かえることをしる

A cloud emerges from a
valley and floats naturally,
gracefully with the wind.

The birds return to their nests
when they are tired.

After all is said and done,
human beings are
a part of nature.

A cloud emerges from between the mountains.

Birds return to their nests and stop
flying when they are tired.
Neither birds nor clouds have ulterior
motives or devious plans.

Clouds float where the wind takes them.
Birds follow time. There is no battle.
There is no give and take.
Floating free in the sky.

This is the meaning of freedom of spirit.

*No matter how much civilization advances, in
the end human beings are part of nature too.*

*Let us try to move around freely, accept
what is in front of us, and live as if
we are flowing, leaving no trace.*

*After all is said and done, everything
is just a small incident in nature.*

話尽山雲海月情

<ruby>話<rt>かたりつくす</rt></ruby><ruby>尽<rt></rt></ruby><ruby>山<rt>さんうんかいげつのじょう</rt></ruby><ruby>雲<rt></rt></ruby><ruby>海<rt></rt></ruby><ruby>月<rt></rt></ruby><ruby>情<rt></rt></ruby>

かたりつくす さんうんかいげつのじょう

Talk of the mountains, the clouds,
the sea and the moon to your
heart's content.

Talk with friends that you can trust with all your heart.

Nature is truth that has been given to us; a truth that we take for granted.

What the mountains tell us, what the clouds tell us, what the seas tell us, what the moon tells us . . . What we feel from nature depends on our heart, as we observe, as we listen.

Fine tune the receptors of your heart, and feel what nature is telling you.

Talk with friends who have grown up in the same environment, friends you trust with all your heart.

Your conversation is sure to flow endlessly, like the clouds that emerge from between the mountains.

只在此山中
ただこのさんちゅうにあり

雲深不知処
くもふこうして ところをしらず

What you seek
may be somewhere in the mountains
but hidden by clouds.

*The fact is, everyone has the heart
of enlightenment within them.*

We all have the pure,
innocent heart we were born with.
But sometimes this heart is obscured by cloud.

Every person possesses the ability
to achieve enlightenment.

To truly achieve an enlightened heart may
seem very difficult. However, an enlightened
heart is not as far away as you think.
It is inside your body, not outside it.
It is merely concealed, by uncertainty,
by the desire for worldly things,
by delusions, by the fog of distraction.

We have lost sight of our pure, innocent hearts.
But if we sweep away the fog,
our heart is right here.

Happiness is here. It is inside us.

Do not laugh in order to get a reaction,
and do not cry in order to get a reaction.
Laugh when you feel like laughing,
and cry when you feel like crying.

Where is the heart that is like that of a baby,
with no pride and no self-consciousness?

That heart exists inside all of us.

破草鞋

<ruby>破<rt>は</rt></ruby><ruby>草<rt>そう</rt></ruby><ruby>鞋<rt>あい</rt></ruby>

Live as though you are a pair
of worn, discarded sandals.

Keep going, do not stop,
even when you reach the limit
known as "nothingness."

Think of a pair of worn-out straw sandals
that are of no use to anyone anymore.

Cut off all distractions, and stand at the
border of nothingness. And then, throw
away what is called *myokyogai*, the limit of
enlightenment. If you are still basking in the
praise of others, you still have some way to go.

Be like a simpleton, in whom others cannot
sense a trace of enlightenment or saintliness.

When you have lost the sense that
you have lost everything, you will
achieve true nothingness.

Live as if you are a useless, broken sandal,
whose existence itself has been forgotten,
yet still exists. That's just about right.

Try to forget everything you've
learned, everything you've built.

And then, pick things up again.

And again, and again, and again.

微風吹幽松

近聴声愈好

びふう ゆうしょうをふく

ちかくきけば こえ いよいよよし

A gentle breeze flows
through the old pine tree.
The closer you get, the more
comforting it sounds.

Look at the things you haven't noticed before.

A gentle breeze blows through
a quiet old pine tree.
That breeze can be heard only when you
stand right next to the tree and listen closely.

When listening to someone else's worries,
it's important be close to that person.
However, instead of sitting opposite each
other, each facing a different direction, the
most important thing is to sit side by side, so
that you are both looking at things from the
same point of view.

The soul does not shout out loud.

People do not shout out their true feelings in loud voices. We have to listen closely to others so that we can understand what they are saying.

If you become a listener, and become able to see things from the same point of view as someone else, only then can you truly understand what that person is feeling.

Sit quietly, and listen.

You will become aware of something that goes beyond the five senses.

吾心似秋月
わがこころ　しゅうげつににたり

碧潭清皎潔
へきたんきょうして　こうけつたり

無物堪比倫
ものの　ひりんにたうるなし

教我如何説
われをして　いかんがとかしめん

Do we really understand the nature
of Buddha, which is like the autumn moon?

Are we clouding the moon that is Buddha
with a fog of worldly desires and distraction?

Are our hearts as pure and clean as the
autumn moon, and as clear as deep blue water?

*A heart that has reached enlightenment
is as peaceful as the autumn moon.*

Try to become aware of the true
heart that hides deep within you.
That true heart is as pure as the autumn
moon, and cannot be described in words.

Try making some waves in your heart
by asking yourself these questions.

What is the meaning of my life?

What is my purpose, my duty?

Ask yourself these questions, which
will make waves in your heart.
When you have calmed those waves, you will
be able see into your heart's deepest place.

You will be able to see a quiet world
that cannot be described in words.

南嶽磨塼

なんがくません

The methods do not matter.

The heart is what is important.
The techniques do not matter.

Long ago, in China, there was a Zen Buddhist monk called Nangaku. One day he saw an apprentice monk called Baso doing Zen meditation very diligently. Nangaku asked him, "What are you trying to achieve by meditating?"

Baso replied, "I am trying to become Buddha."

Nangaku started to polish a roof tile. Baso asked, "What are you trying to achieve?"

"I'm trying to polish the tile to make it into a mirror," replied Nangaku.

"A roof tile will not become a mirror by polishing it," said Baso.

To that, Nangaku said, "In the same way, you cannot become Buddha just because you do Zen meditation."

*Do not get caught up in the "form" of
Zen meditation, believing that this will
help you achieve a "Zen" state.*

*What is important is the heart.
Zen meditation techniques are not important.
Your heart needs to be fully engaged.*

*This lesson can also be applied to the way
you live your life. If you are too caught up in
the method you are using to do something,
you will eventually lose sight of the goal.*

*What is the real goal?
What is our true nature?*

Remember to ask yourself these questions.

They will bring peace to your heart.

堪対暮雲帰未合
遠山無限碧層層

たいするにたえたり　ぼうんのかえっていまだがっせざるに
えんざんかぎりなき　へきぞうぞう

The mountains glimpsed
through the evening clouds
continue in layers of green forever.

*Make every day important, for we do
not know what tomorrow will bring.*

On a late autumn evening, the mountains
are shrouded in red-tinged sunset clouds.
Glimpsed between the clouds are layers
of mountains, high and low, stretching
on and on, as far as the eye can see.

On life's long journey, we do not
know what tomorrow will bring.
We don't know if tomorrow will come at all.

That is why every day is the twilight of life.

Was I able to live today without any regrets?

Did I come home at the end of the day having achieved what I set out to do?

Did I live today as best I could?

Constantly ask your heart these questions.

Winter

Every day is a positive day.

Even bad days are valuable.

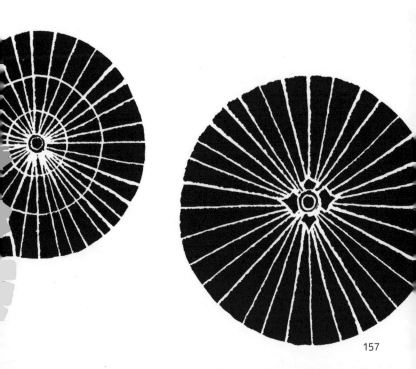

A "positive" day in this Zen saying
does not mean a "good day."
It means a "day of value" in our lives.

We all have sad days, when it's impossible
to have smiles on our faces.

There are those painful days when we must
say goodbye forever to our loved ones,
as they embark on the eternal journey.

Not every day is "good." That's life.

But nor is every day "bad."

Even if sad events continue, we can always try to turn them into positive experiences, and they can change into positive memories.

Bad days may eventually turn into good days. Bad relationships may turn into good ones.

Be someone who can make those things happen. Live today the best you can.

When you are sad, be sad with all your heart. When you are angry, be angry with all your heart. When you laugh, laugh with all your heart.

Live well. Don't waste the day that is today. This is what it means to live.

好雪片片不落別処

こうせつへんぺん べっしょにおちず

Snowflakes are beautiful,
and they all fall in their
proper places.

Do not be afraid.
Live while accepting everything.

Snowflakes fall from the heavens
one by one, falling where they should,
in their proper places.
They all fall exactly where they should.

In the same way, the moments of sadness and
hardship in life fall in their proper places.
They fall exactly where they should.

Don't try to avoid sadness or hardship.
Accept these difficulties.

As death cannot be avoided, confront
it face to face, and treasure the
time you have left in life.

Receive everything as you would receive a
single snowflake in your hand, without fear.

吾道一以貫之

<ruby>吾<rt>わ</rt></ruby><ruby>道<rt>が</rt></ruby>

わがどういつもって これをつらぬく

I have always lived my life
according to one principle.

Do each thing thoughtfully.

Instead of getting obsessed with just one thing, treat all the things that are in front of you with care. That is what it means to live according to one principle.

Cook, eat, clean, do the laundry, work, play with your children, enjoy your hobbies, sleep.

When you pour your heart into each of those things the path you should take is revealed to you.

If you find the path you need to take while having fun, then this can truly be called enjoyment.

Even if you encounter unpleasant things, or things you don't want to do, don't switch off. Keep your heart switched on.

Treasure every thing that presents itself to you, and live your life to its fullest.

紅炉上一点雪

<ruby>こうろじょういってんのゆき</ruby>

A single snowflake
on a red-hot coal.

Live this day to its fullest.

A snowflake falls gently on a red hot coal.
The snowflake disappears in an
instant, leaving no trace.

Death comes to every one of us,
and afterward, we simply fade away.

From the moment a person is born,
they are heading toward death.

Because we live while heading toward death, we should live as fully as we can.

Discard your obsession with staying alive. Discard your fear of dying.

Keep your heart calm, and keep living while heading toward death.

Live in the present, as best you can. Live for today.

松樹千年翠
不入時人意

しょうじゅせんねんのみどり
ときのひとこころにいらず

The evergreen of the pine tree
goes unnoticed.

*Just as the green of the pine
tree does not fade,
what a person has gained
in their life never fades.*

The green of the pine tree does not fade.

In winter, when the leaves of other trees have all fallen, the branches of the pine tree are greenest. That color is not created in a single day.

In the same way, the knowledge and experience that a person has accumulated during a lifetime is not something that fades away.

If you have lived your life like the eternal pine tree, pass on your knowledge and experience to the next generation with generosity.

And if you are of the younger generation, don't wait to be taught; turn your heart toward the sources of knowledge, and absorb that knowledge as your own.

The pine tree is right there.

応無所住而生其心

まさにじゅうするところなくして そのこころをしょうずべし

Do not become too
fixated on one thing;
let your heart roam free.

You do not need "belief,"
if that belief means
your heart can no
longer move freely.

Don't let "beliefs" capture your susceptible heart. These could be beliefs that say you must live in a certain way, or that a certain method will help you win.

But the stronger and more rigid the belief, the more completely it will shatter.

Try not to fixate on a particular belief. This will allow the heart to become freer, to roam around with abandon. Never putting your whole heart into one particular belief means that your heart is always present, everywhere.

If you can achieve this natural state, your heart will become strong and steadfast.

Imagine a column supporting your heart. If it is too straight, the column can easily be shaken. Let your heart move freely.

Eliminate the beliefs that try to shove you into a small, tight space.

Do not let your life become poorer due to rigid beliefs.

把手共行

<ruby>把<rt>て</rt></ruby><ruby>手<rt>をとって</rt></ruby><ruby>共<rt>ともに</rt></ruby><ruby>行<rt>ゆく</rt></ruby>

Walk together, holding hands.

You do not live in solitude.

Happiness does not necessarily mean
that you yourself become happy.
Happiness comes when you can
make someone else happy.
Happiness means to walk with others.

Happiness does not mean
being controlled by dreams and aspirations.
It means living together with your true self.

Happiness is right there.

Even when the time comes to say goodbye
forever to a precious person in your life,
think of the things that brought that person joy,
the things that made that person laugh,
the things that person taught you,
the things that person scolded you for,
the things that you learned from that person.
You will continue living with all those things,
even after that person is gone.

Partings are inevitable in life, but the people
who leave us continue to live on in our hearts.

They continue to live with us, together, forever.

看脚下

かんきゃっか

Do not lose sight of your feet.

When in doubt, look at your feet.

When walking in the dark at night,
a light is your biggest ally.
But if the light goes out, what can you do?

When we lose a teacher who showed us the
way, or when we lose a partner at whose side
we walked through life, what should we do?

There's no need to be lost.

*At those times, all you need to do
is look down at your feet.*

*Instead of worrying about what will
happen to you from now on, look closely
at where you stand, at this moment.
Keep your feet firmly on the ground.
In this way you can continue living.*

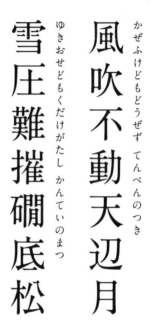

風吹不動天辺月
雪圧難摧澗底松

The moon does not move,
even when the wind blows.

The pine in the valley does not break,
even when there is heavy snow.

188

What we want to have is a spirit that does not break, even in the most difficult circumstances.

The moon in the sky above does not
move when the wind blows.

The pine tree, battered by the elements,
does not break when snow falls on it.
It simply flicks away the snow,
preserving its bright green branches.

*With your inner strength you
can endure any difficulty.*

*When you are visited by hardship,
think of the pride of the pine tree.*

*Remember the pine tree and how it
doesn't change color or wither away,
even if it is covered with snow.*

Think of the quiet strength of the pine tree.

巌谷栽松
<ruby>巌<rt>がん</rt></ruby><ruby>谷<rt>こく</rt></ruby><ruby>栽<rt>さい</rt></ruby><ruby>松<rt>しょう</rt></ruby>

Plant pine trees in
the deep valley.

After running the distance
as hard as you can,
pass the baton to the next runner.

Plant trees in the bare, rugged
landscape deep in the mountains.
Not to gain praise.
Not to insist that others do the same.

If people see the pine trees you have
planted with a sure heart, and see
what you were thinking, and continue
what you did, that is enough.

Life is not a short distance race
that you run on your own.

Life is a relay race.

*After running your stage of the
race as hard as you can,
it's fine to just collapse.*

*Someone who has seen you running
as hard as you can will take the baton
from you and continue the race.*

*There is no need to push your
opinions onto others.*

*All we need to do is show those who come
after us that we have lived as best we could.*

山中無暦日
<ruby>山<rt>さん</rt></ruby><ruby>中<rt>ちゅう</rt></ruby><ruby>無<rt>に</rt></ruby><ruby>暦<rt>れきじつ</rt></ruby><ruby>日<rt>なし</rt></ruby>

There is no calendar
in the mountains.

Make some time when you can be "nothing."

When you are in the mountains, where it is
quietness itself, you lose track of the months
and of the days of the week.

When you are in a place where you
are no longer bound by the limits of
time, your heart is gently untangled.

Try separating yourself just a little
bit from the noise of society.

Try to have some "time in the mountains"
in your own way, cutting off
all that is unnecessary.

When you feel happy and joyful
that itself is nothingness.

A person's heart becomes stronger when
it lives on the border of nothingness.

擔雪填古井

ゆきをにのうて こせいをうずむ

Fill an old well with snow.

Don't look for immediate rewards.
Keep striving forever, toward that eternal goal.

There is no need to be too occupied
with being efficient and rational.

Sometimes it's fine to try something silly,
like filling up an old well with snow.

*Don't expect to produce results
immediately. Don't expect to receive
a response immediately.*

*Don't complain about the meaning
of doing something.*

*Don't complain that it's useless
to try to find peace.*

*There is meaning in just carrying on,
believing in what you are doing.*

Even if it is just a small action.

百尺竿頭進一歩

ひゃくしゃくかんとうに いっぽをすすむ

When you have reached the end
of the long pole, take another step.

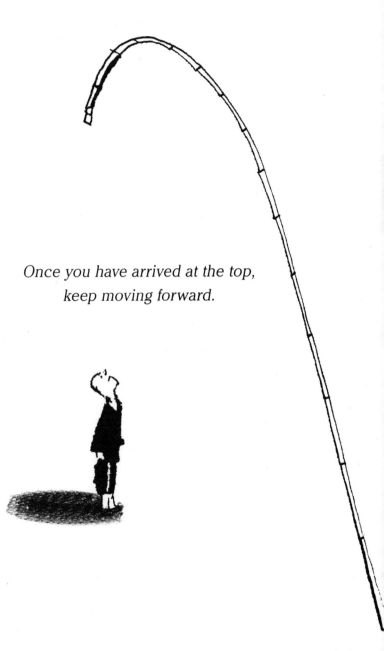

Once you have arrived at the top,
keep moving forward.

It feels so good to reach a goal in life.

But don't just stop there.
Once you have reached the end of that
long, long pole, try taking one more step.

If you take that step from the very top,
you will probably fall, but don't be afraid.
Just think of it as returning from
the top of the mountain.

Just think of it as coming down
from the top of the mountain.

Don't just use what you have
learned for yourself.
Your knowledge only has meaning
when you can use it for society as a whole.

Once you have reached the top,
brace yourself, and take a step
beyond that place of comfort.

百雑砕
<ruby>百<rt>ひゃく</rt></ruby><ruby>雑<rt>ざっ</rt></ruby><ruby>砕<rt>さい</rt></ruby>

Destroy everything.

Don't be afraid of loss.

When you become attached to things,
you start to fear losing them.
If you become too obsessed with position
or reputation, you become stuck.

Throw away your obsessions and
your attachments bravely.

Smash them into tiny pieces.

*Pass your position in society and reputation
to the people who come after you,
and forget about these things.*

That's the spirit.

*Once you have smashed everything into
pieces, your heart will be free.*

林下十年夢
りんかじゅうねんのゆめ

湖辺一笑新
こへんいっしょうあらたなり

After ten years of hard
training in the forest,
I stood on the edge
of the lake
and laughed anew
with all my might.

Life starts again, from this point.

You've worked so hard until now.

You worked hard at your job, and
retired from your company.
You worked hard to bring up your children,
and now they've left home and married.

The long period of training has ended,
and your heart is now light and happy.
You have done good work.

But this is not the end.

*After completing one phase of training,
we come to a new starting point.
Life begins anew.*

This is the first chapter of the rest of your life.

活溌溌地
<ruby>活<rt>かっ</rt></ruby>

かっぱっぱっち

Be alert and full of energy.

Be open to new discoveries every day.

That food that you think is delicious the first time you try it loses its novelty, and even its flavor, if you eat it every day. The scenery you think is beautiful the first time you see it looks ordinary if you gaze at it every day.

If you have too much knowledge and experience, your heart stops dancing with joy.

Try emptying your heart.
Because there is no day that's exactly like yesterday.

The way you commute to work every day; the view outside your window that you see every day: even in those mundane things there are new discoveries to be made every day.

Think back to that alert tension you felt the first time you finished a work project.

Remember the confusion you felt when you started living on your own for the first time.

Instead of feeling that you've done or seen it all before, look for the newness in every moment.

Those fresh emotions that you've forgotten about are right here, right now.

Epilogue

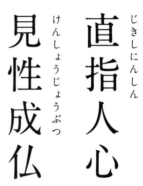

直指人心
見性成仏

じきしにんしん
けんしょうじょうぶつ

Look directly inside yourself
to find the Buddha.

*In the end, you can only look
directly into your own heart.*

These are the fundamental teachings
of Zen Buddhism, according to the
great Zen Buddhist monk Daruma:

Value experience over words.

Enlightenment is transmitted
from heart to heart.

Real truth is not found outside you;
it is within you.

In order to see the truth inside you,
you must become Buddha yourself.

Life's answers are not to be gained by asking others, and getting them to teach you. Life's answers cannot be communicated with words.

The questions to be asked are from your own heart, to be understood through your own body.

*The answers given by others
are merely opinions.*

Question yourself, and look directly into your own heart. Think things through carefully by yourself. The answers that you feel when you do this are the truth.

To live a life without regrets, the only thing you can do is to find your own answers, and keep moving forward.

Happiness is right in front of you

Zen Buddhism is not a kind of magic that makes something exist that wasn't there before. If, after reading this book, you see the world in a new way, that's because your perception of the world has changed.

From the age of 22 to 31, I trained to become a Buddhist monk. I spent every day meditating and studying, trying to achieve enlightenment. But after those nine years I didn't feel I'd gained anything new or that Zen had changed me. But I did realize there is a season for everything. I did not even notice this before, as I was so used to my everyday comforts. My training helped me to appreciate something that I had overlooked.

Zen meditation is a way of throwing away all the accumulated trash in your heart. This book can help you do this. I hope you will continue to use this book to get a fresh look at your "self." When we feel gratitude for the daily things we take for granted we can find the happiness we had in our hearts all along. The teachings of Zen are all road signs that point to that destination.

Zen Buddhist master Hakuin Ekaku said: "This very place is the land of the lotus, and this very body is Buddha." This means, if you think of the place you are now as the best place to be, then your life will overflow with happiness.

In conclusion, what I can communicate to you is just one thing. Happiness is always right in front of you. If this book helps you live with a full, abundant heart in even a small way, nothing would make me happier, as an author and as a Zen Buddhist priest.

—Shinsuke Hosokawa